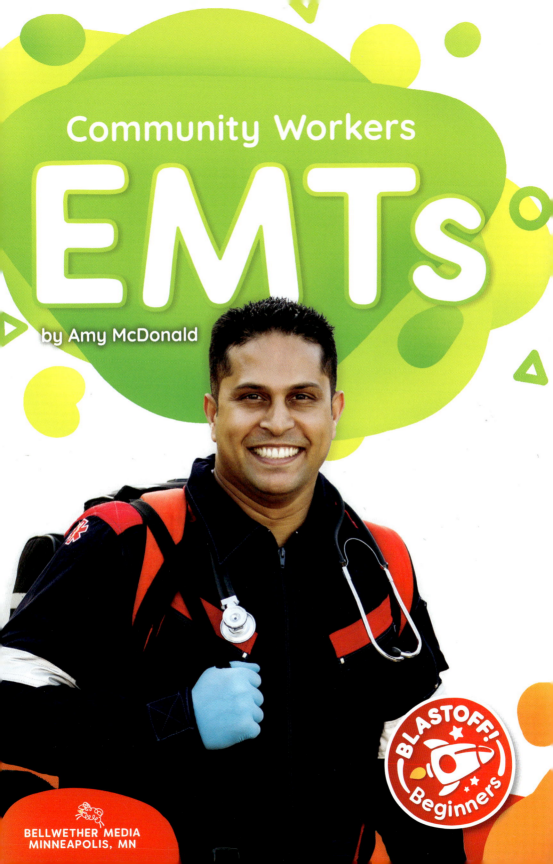

Community Workers

EMTs

by Amy McDonald

BLASTOFF! Beginners

BELLWETHER MEDIA
MINNEAPOLIS, MN

Blastoff! Beginners are developed by literacy experts and educators to meet the needs of early readers. These engaging informational texts support young children as they begin reading about their world. Through simple language and high frequency words paired with crisp, colorful photos, Blastoff! Beginners launch young readers into the universe of independent reading.

Sight Words in This Book

and	here	time
are	in	to
called	is	we
first	on	
for	people	
help	they	

This edition first published in 2025 by Bellwether Media, Inc.

No part of this publication may be reproduced in whole or in part without written permission of the publisher. For information regarding permission, write to Bellwether Media, Inc., Attention: Permissions Department, 6012 Blue Circle Drive, Minnetonka, MN 55343.

Library of Congress Cataloging-in-Publication Data

LC record for EMTs available at: https://lccn.loc.gov/2024038072

Text copyright © 2025 by Bellwether Media, Inc. BLASTOFF! BEGINNERS and associated logos are trademarks and/or registered trademarks of Bellwether Media, Inc.

Editor: Betsy Rathburn   Designer: Laura Sowers

Printed in the United States of America, North Mankato, MN.

Table of Contents

On the Job	4
What Are They?	6
What Do They Do?	10
Why Do We Need Them?	20
EMT Facts	22
Glossary	23
To Learn More	24
Index	24

On the Job

Someone is hurt.
We called 911.
Help is here!

What Are They?

EMTs are emergency medical technicians.

They drive **ambulances**. They work in cities and towns.

ambulance

What Do They Do?

EMTs answer calls for help. They move fast.

They help sick or hurt people. They give **first aid**.

They put people on **stretchers**.

stretcher

They drive people to **emergency rooms.**

They help during scary times.
They stay calm.

Why Do We Need Them?

EMTs save lives!

EMT Facts

Tools

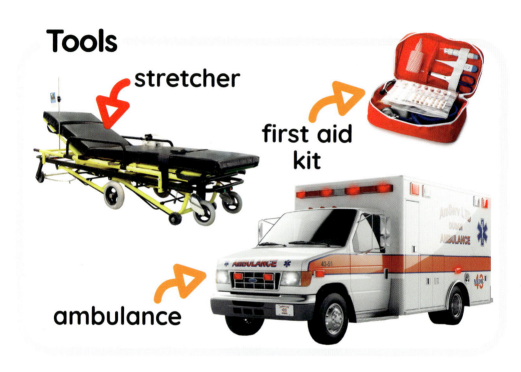

- stretcher
- first aid kit
- ambulance

A Day in the Life

answer calls for help

give first aid

drive people to emergency rooms

Glossary

ambulances

vehicles used for medical emergencies

emergency rooms

parts of hospitals where people get help quickly

first aid

help given to sick or hurt people

stretchers

tools for carrying sick or hurt people

To Learn More

ON THE WEB

FACTSURFER

Factsurfer.com gives you a safe, fun way to find more information.

1. Go to www.factsurfer.com.

2. Enter "EMTs" into the search box and click 🔍.

3. Select your book cover to see a list of related content.

Index

911, 4	first aid, 12	towns, 8
ambulances, 8	help, 4, 10, 12, 18	work, 8
calls, 10	hurt, 4, 12	
calm, 18	people, 12, 14, 16	
cities, 8	sick, 12	
drive, 8, 16	stretchers, 14	
emergency rooms, 16, 17		

The images in this book are reproduced through the courtesy of: michaeljung, front cover, pp. 14-15; Leonid Smirnov, p. 3; kali9, pp. 4-5, 18-19, 23 (first aid); Peakstock, pp. 6-7; Rob Wilson, p. 8; Alex Potemkin, pp. 8-9; ZUMA Press Inc/Alamy, p. 10; Tyler Olson, pp. 10-11; Vitte Yevhen, p. 12; valentinrussanov, pp. 12-13; Vereshchagin Dmitry, pp. 14, 22 (stretcher); Rob Hainer, p. 16; FangXiaNuo, pp. 16-17, 20; CandyBox Images, pp. 20-21; New Africa, p. 22 (first aid kit); Quad Design, p. 22 (ambulance); Photoroyalty, p. 22 (answer calls for help); Kzenon, p. 22 (give first aid); Stefan Malloch, p. 22 (drive people to emergency rooms); Venturelli Luca, p. 23 (ambulances); Dolores M. Harvey, p. 23 (emergency rooms); Steve Sanchez Photos, p. 23 (stretchers).